Awesome Riddles And Trick Questions For Kids

Puzzling Questions and Fun Facts

For Ages 5 to 8

With
Fun Illustrations

Riddleland

Table of Contents

bonus book

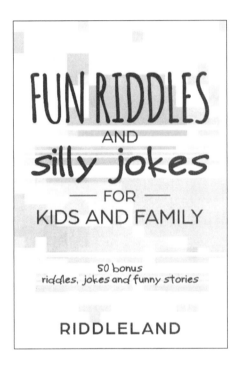

SCAN ME

https://pixelfy.me/riddlelandbonus

Thank you for buying this book. We would like to share
a special bonus as a token of appreciation.
It is a collection of 50 original jokes, riddles, and
two funny stories

Introduction

"Play is often talked about as if it were a relief from serious learning. But for children, play is serious learning."

~ Mr. Rogers

We would like to thank you for picking up a copy of this book. Awesome Riddles for Kids Ages 5-8 is a collection of fun riddles, trick questions, and brain teasers that will get kids interested in learning through play.

As parents, we want our children to do the very best in life they can, and we understand that a good education is instrumental to their future success. We wrote this riddle book to help our children learn in a fun way. Our key belief is that learning can and should be fun and enjoyable, and we hope that after reading and using this book with your family, you'll agree.

Riddles are perfect for 5-8 year olds because having fun riddles to work out is great for beginner readers or older children who are developing their reading habit. Riddles are quick and easy to read, making this a great book to dip in and out of when time permits.

Riddles are a great way to engage children of this age, and as well as being fun, thought-provoking, and entertaining they have a whole host of other benefits:

- **Children can improve their vocabulary and learn new words.**

- **Through the 'What am I?' or 'What is it?' style of questions, children can learn how things are described.**

- **With each word they read, they learn more about reading, phonetics, and pronunciation, plus gaining confidence in reading aloud to others.**

- **Riddles engage children's curiosity. The riddles get them thinking, working things out, looking at problems from different perspectives, developing and a questioning independent mind, all of which are great skills for the future.**

Finally, the riddles can be an excellent way to encourage families to spend quality time together reading, asking questions, listening to responses, and having fun.

The book includes 'what am I?' questions, tricky scenarios, guess the word, and anagram sections, which will help children with spelling and increasing vocabulary. There are also fun facts in the book too.

We hope you enjoy the riddles as much as our children did. We, as parents, enjoyed seeing our children thinking and learning while having fun.

Chapter 1

Awesome Things You Can Find Around You

"The beautiful thing about **LEARNING** is that no one can take it away **FROM YOU.**"

Chapter 1 - Questions

1. I have so many words. Sometimes I can tell a wonderful story. Other times, I can tell you an incredible fact. You can use me to read, or you can use me to write.

What am I ?

2. I walk on four legs, and I am really friendly. So friendly in fact, that I am sometimes kept in houses. I love to lick people's faces and run around and play!

What am I ?

3. I can hold things and I can lift things too. Without me, you won't be able to take things from one place to another. I also split into five smaller parts. I am always with you.

What am I ?

4. I live in your body. I can race, but I am not in your legs. I am steady if you are calm and I am fast if you are nervous. I help blood flow throughout your body.

What am I ?

Chapter 1 - Questions

5. Leave me alone, and I do not grow. Take away more of me and I get bigger.

What am I ?

6. You can find me in many different colors. I am quite beautiful, and some people like to pick my petals. I can be found in a garden or inside a small container. I can be used as a gift.

What am I ?

7. I like to hop, but I am not a rabbit. I am not even a kangaroo. I do not have a tail. You can find me near a pond.

What am I ?

8. You can find me in many colors. I get big when I eat air. If you don't hold me, then I might fly away. If you break me, then I can make a loud sound.

What am I ?

Chapter 1 - Questions

9. Sometimes, I have a small body, and sometimes I have a large body. I may have many doors, or I may have few doors. People paint me and they decorate me. Sometimes, people invite their friends and other times, they like to be alone.

What am I ?

10. You should use me carefully since I can be quite sharp. I can be used for making wonderful art. I can also be used to cut hair! Keep me steady in your hands, and do not run around while holding me.

What am I ?

11. I usually come in pairs. Sometimes you can tie me, other times you can strap me. If you are stepping outside, then you might need me. Don't go splashing in water without me.

What am I ?

12. I am capable of holding a lot of water, even though I have many holes!

What am I ?

13. I am quite hot, and I don't live on the ground. In fact, you can see me in the sky. I may look small, but in reality, I am a giant ball of fire. When it is nighttime, you won't see me.

What am I ?

14. I am a really tasty treat. You can find me in a cup, or you can add me into a cone. You can sprinkle me with lots of sweet stuff. I can be fruit flavored, or I can be chocolate.

What am I ?

FUN FACT

The first food that was taken into space and eaten by astronauts was applesauce.

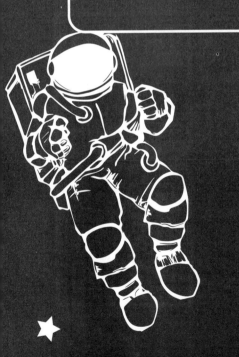

15. I always go up, and I never come down. I make people grow up as well.

What am I ?

16. When you are resting, then you can use me. Your head and your neck find comfort with me.

What am I ?

17. You can use me to watch entertainment. I can be placed on a shelf, or I can be hung on the wall. You should use a remote to control me.

What am I ?

18. I can have a zipper, but I can also have buttons. You might not need me during summer, but you need me during winter. I keep you warm. Sometimes, I can protect you from the rain.

What am I ?

19. I have four fingers and a thumb, but I have holes as well! I am not alive.

What am I ?

20. You won't be able to throw me. However, you can definitely catch me.

What am I ?

21. When you are sick, you have me. I am not easy to get. I come in many different forms. You have to go to a doctor if you need to find me.

What am I ?

22. I may not be able to open any doors, but I still have a lot of keys. Use one key, and a different tune plays.

What am I ?

FUN FACT

It may not look like it, but in each ear of a cat, there are 32 muscles !

23. I am always falling down. I never move up. If the sky is clear, you will never find me.

What am I ?

24. I may be a ball, but I cannot be thrown. I don't bounce up or down Instead, I am very useful to you.

What am I ?

25. Use me to hold something hot or something cold. I usually come with a small handle.

What am I ?

26. I am able to jump. I am able to climb. I can walk up the walls. I can walk down a very thin string. Oh, and did I tell you that I made the string?

What am I ?

Chapter 1 - Questions

27. I go round and round. I move up and down. I can be thrown easily, but you can also catch me easily. Just don't throw me at objects because I can break them.

What am I ?

28. When things are wet, I am stay dry. But when they are drying, I get wet.

What am I ?

Chapter 1 - Questions

29. Every time you take a bath, I get smaller and smaller. I come in different shapes. I also have different smells.

What am I ?

30. You have to break me to use me. I can be eaten in many ways.

What am I ?

31. I have a face, but I cannot see or hear. I do have hands, but I cannot use them to clap.

What am I ?

32. I do not have a head, but I have a long neck.

What am I ?

FUN FACT

The word 'stewardesses' is the longest word that you can type using only one hand – your left hand!

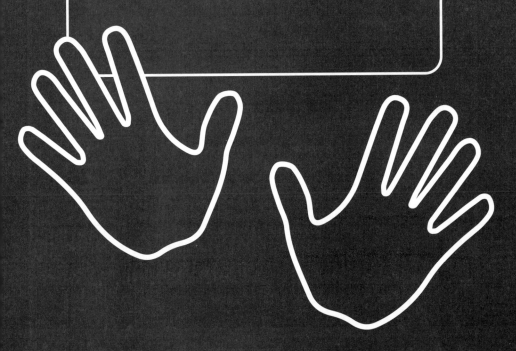

33. I have four legs, but I am not an animal. I have one head, and a foot, but I am not alive.

What am I ?

34. I have many teeth, but I don't use them to chew food. You can hold me in your hand.

What am I ?

35. When I walk, I am jumping. When I stand, I am actually sitting. I have a tail.

What am I ?

36. My back is straight, but I have many teeth. I am often used for cutting.

What am I ?

Chapter 1 - Questions

37. I have the color brown. I have the color green. If you give me plenty of water, I can live for a long time. I am the house for many birds. Some people like to climb me.

What am I ?

38. I am found in front of doors, and I am quite soft. I don't move, and I can be quite hairy too.

What am I ?

39. You see me at night. Even though you can see me with the naked eye, I am not close enough for you to touch. I am quite far away.

What am I ?

40. I have a tail. I also have a head. But I do not have arms or legs.

What am I ?

Chapter 1 - Questions

41. I do not walk, but I run a lot. When I move forward, you are not far behind.

What am I ?

42. I cry without any eyes and fly without wing.

What am I ?

43. I am a nut with a hole in the center. I am usually sweet.

What am I ?

44. If I point up, then there is no light. But when I am point down, you have light.

What am I ?

45. I am a juicy fruit, but I have seeds on the outside.

What am I ?

46. There are just two eyes on my head, but there are plenty more on my tail.

What am I ?

47. I am worn around the neck and I come in different colors. Some people prefer to have me with spots, but others like stripes. There are many who don't like any design at all.

What am I ?

FUN FACT

Vatican City is the smallest country in the world. It is only about 5 square kilometers.

saint peter's basilica

5 square kilometers

48. I am usually white, but I come in different colors. You can create fantastic pictures on me, or you can use me to show words. I can be folded as well, if you would like to make shapes out of me.

What am I ?

49. I have legs, but I cannot walk. I do keep you warm. I can be quite thin, or I can be pretty thick.

What am I ?

50. I help pants stay up, and I also help engines go round and round.

What am I ?

51. I can flip and I can leap. I can flex and I can perform incredible tricks.

Who am I ?

52. Many people wear me. I protect your eyes from the sun.

What am I ?

53. You can find me on water, but I am not a living thing. In fact, I am something people use. I bob up and down if things get a little wavy. I am kept close to the shore, so I don't drift away.

What am I ?

Chapter 1 - Questions

54. I can be as small as an insect, and as big as a building. But I do not weigh anything. In fact, I am usually follow you around.

What am I ?

55. I can hold objects, but I usually hold food. When people want to eat something, they use me. I am circular in shape and come in many colors.

What am I ?

56. I can make people wake up in the morning. But I am not an alarm or a machine. I do have wings and a pair of legs.

What am I ?

57. I swing from tree to tree. I am pretty hairy. I can be big, or I can be small. Oh, and I do love bananas.

What am I ?

Chapter 1 - Questions

58. When I am young, I am quite tall. When I am old however, I become really short. I can burn bright, but you have to light me.

What am I ?

59. I am able to run, even though I have no legs. I usually flow downwards, and I join a bigger body. I can branch out as well.

What am I ?

60. When you see more of me, you see less of the world. I am present more during the night than during the day.

What am I ?

61. You may be able to find me in a hamburger, or you could find me in a soup. I can be found in a stew, but I am usually chopped into small pieces. When I am raw, I am the color green. But when I become ripe, I turn red! People used to think I was a vegetable, but I am a fruit.

What am I ?

FUN FACT

Did you know that in Iceland, there are certain ice caves that have springs? That does not sound surprising now does it? Here is the best part. These springs are hot springs!

Chapter 1 - Questions

62. Usually you find me in a corner. I can visit many places in the world. I can reach the farthest country in the east all the way to the far corners of the west!

What am I ?

63. I have a long neck and many spots on my body. I like to eat plants and I can easily reach the tops of many trees. If you come close to me, then don't worry, I am quite gentle.

What am I ?

64. Look up, and you will be able to find me. I have a glow, which gives you light in dark places. When you wake up in the morning, I won't be there. Don't worry. I am still here. Wait until the evening, and you will be able to see me again.

What am I ?

65. You cannot enter me, even though I am in a room. I have a large top, but I am not a tree. You can add me to your soup, or you can add me to a stew. I can taste quite delicious but be careful since some of me are poisonous.

What am I ?

66. You can throw me, but I usually turn around and come back to you. Usually I have a bent body.

What am I ?

67. You do not find me with arms, and I do not have a head. But guess what, you need me when you want to keep warm or cover yourself. I can look plain, or I can look stylish.

What am I ?

68. I have only one leg, but I have three eyes. If I open one eye, then everything stops. When I open a different eye, then I can tell things to start moving. Each of my eyes is a different color.

What am I ?

69. I have many arms, but they never meet. I can wave at you, but I create cool air when I do so. You usually need me when you feel hot.

What am I ?

70. If you cut me, then you end up crying. I am quite important when you are making a lot of food. You can find me between slices of bread, or you can add me to gravy.

What am I ?

71. I am present as long as you don't say anything. Even saying my name can break me. I am quite fragile, I tell you.

What am I ?

72. I help cure your cold. I help you fight infections. I check your heart, and I look into your eyes. I want to help you get better.

Who am I ?

73. People give me away, but many people need me. I have different numbers on my face. The more of me you have, the more you can buy. I can fit into your pocket. I can be paper, or I can be metal.

What am I ?

FUN FACT

Did you know that your body also gives off a certain amount of light? However, you cannot see it with the naked eye,and you need special instrument scalled "infrared detectors" to catch this light.

74. I am attached to a string, but I am not found on the ground. I may not have wings, but when it gets windy, I can fly. Do be careful that you don't get me tangled up!

What am I ?

75. Close your eyes and I might seem real. I create fantastical worlds, or I make you remember things that already happened to you. When you open your eyes, then I am no longer there.

What am I ?

Chapter 1 - Questions

76. You can only hear me, and you can never see me. But sometimes, when you hear me, you can say to whom I belong. I help you speak words and I help you sing.

What am I ?

77. I live in houses and many buildings. I am there there to help you see or I can be used to make your room bright. Sometimes I am quite strong but other times I break easily.

What am I ?

78. I am usually sour, but I can sometimes be sweet. If you squeeze me, then I can create a wonderful juice. You can have me anytime, but I am usually found during breakfast. I am a healthy source of Vitamin C.

What am I ?

79. I am a small piece of land, but you won't be able to find me easily near you. In fact, if you want to walk on me, then you might have to catch me floating on water.

What am I ?

80. I have a long tail and long nails. I live in your in your walls and I make skittering noises. Most people don't like me in their houses. I am definitely not invited into the kitchen. I do have a furry coat, but you should try to stay away from me.

What am I ?

81. I am sparkly, but I am not glitter. If things are hot outside, then you won't see me. But when it gets chilly, you might be able to catch me. Each one of me is unique.

What am I ?

82. I float in space, but I am not an object. I have been to the moon. If you would like to see Mars, then you would need me.

Who am I ?

83. I like to stay on the farm, but I am not a cow. I have a fluffy coat. In fact, you use my coat to make your clothes!

What am I ?

84. I can hold so much information. The sharper I am, the more of me you can use. I can help you remember. You need me to solve this riddle book!

What am I ?

85. I am usually found in a classroom. I am used to spread knowledge, but I am not a book. I am usually clean until someone starts to write on me.

What am I ?

FUN FACT

Your body sheds its outer layer just like snakes do. Every year, you lose about 4 kilograms of skin cells! But don't worry because new ones are formed as soon as the old ones leave your body.

4 KG

86. I love to go from flower to flower. After I have visited enough flowers, I can make a sweet liquid that many people enjoy. I am important for the planet and I make buzzing noises.

87. I just entered this world. I do not know much about it. Most of the time, you can find me crying. People like to pinch my cheeks. I love milk a lot.

Who am I ?

88. I use a black surface, but I don't create anything out of it. I like to spread knowledge. People look at me when I speak, but I enjoy interacting.

Who am I ?

89. I have a tail and a big mouth. I can swim in water and I can come out on land. I can be pretty scary, and animals run away from me.

What am I ?

90. I use words to create stories. But I can also use words to spread information. I can create make believe worlds, and I can describe real-life stories.

Who am I ?

91. I love to draw and create art. I have a few tools that are unique to me. I have a paintbrush, and I have an easel.

Who am I ?

92. I slither and slide on the ground. I do not have legs, but I can still move around quite quickly. People stay away from me when they see me. You wouldn't want to get bitten by me!

What am I ?

93. I am in your body, and there are two of me. I am shaped like a bean, and I take care of waste.

What am I ?

FUN FACT

Did you know that both parrots and rabbits can see what is behind them without even turning their heads?

94. I am white, but I am not the snow. I am present inside your body, but I am not a liquid. I am a strong substance and I am present from your head to your toe.

What am I ?

95. I was crawling once, but then I could fly. I come in different colors and I stay near flowers. I am beautiful. And no, I don't bite!

What am I ?

96. I am present on both sides of your head. I look like tiny wings, but I don't make you fly. If you need to listen to your favorite music, then you definitely need my help.

What am I ?

97. I start inside a tiny seed. Once I grow up, I am usually green. I may have many hands, or I may have a few.

What am I ?

Chapter 1 - Questions

98. I paint my face, but I make it look funny. Sometimes I have a colored wig, sometimes I do not. Most of all, I like to make people laugh.

Who am I ?

99. I am a ruler, but I am not the King. I am a woman of beauty and power. I give commands and people listen to me.

Who am I ?

Chapter 1 - Questions

100. I have a big snout and I swim in the sea. I am kind of a fish and people love to see me. I can jump into the air and I am quite playful.

What am I ?

101. If your pet has a problem, then you come to me. In fact, I like to take care of all animals. From birds to mammals, from reptiles to fishes.

Who am I ?

102. I aim for the net because that is where my goal is. I cannot touch the ball, but I can kick it around as much as I want. I need to score the most points for my team.

Who am I ?

103. I am called the King, but I am not a human being. I live in the wild and I have a big mane. I do have a big roar and it is a sound that many people can identify.

Who am I ?

104. You don't find me in the city, but you find me in the desert. I am not an animal, but I am a living thing. I can be quite prickly, and you shouldn't touch me. But I am eaten by camels whenever they are hungry.

What am I ?

105. I travel in a car with blue and red lights. I am protecting people in the neighborhood. I usually wear a uniform and I love to greet people.

Who am I ?

Chapter 1 - Questions

106. You can find me in the kitchen. I am always cooking something nice. I like to create unique food. I do wear a hat, but it is usually white.

Who am I ?

107. I like to create music with my voice. Sometimes, I might have a deep voice, sometimes I might have a high-pitched voice. I can create many different tunes.

Who am I ?

108. I am present on your body, but not everywhere. There are millions and millions of me. Sometimes, I am long while other times, I am short. For some people, I can appear on the chin.

What am I ?

109. You can find me in a court, but not the one where they play tennis. I am usually showing facts and defending the innocent. I uphold the law and I am there to punish the guilty.

Who am I ?

FUN FACT

Did you know that all fruit loops have the same flavor? Next time when you have it for breakfast, try each color with your eyes closed.

Guess who or what I am ?

Chapter 1 - Answers

1. A Book	**8.** A Balloon	**15.** Age
2. A Dog	**9.** A House	**16.** A Pillow
3. Your hand	**10.** A Pair of Scissors	**17.** A Television
4. Your heart	**11.** A Pair of Shoes	**18.** A Coat
5. A Hole	**12.** A Sponge	**19.** A Glove
6. A Flower	**13.** The Sun	**20.** A Cold
7. A Frog	**14.** Ice Cream	**21.** A Medicine

22. A Piano	**29.** A Soap	**36.** A Saw
23. Rain	**30.** An Egg	**37.** A Tree
24. Eyeball	**31.** A Clock	**38.** A Carpet
25. A Cup	**32.** A Bottle	**39.** Stars
26. A Spider	**33.** A Bed	**40.** A Coin
27. A Ball	**34.** A Comb	**41.** Your Nose (Runny
28. A Towel	**35.** A Kangaroo	nose, get it)

42. A Cloud	**49.** Pants	**56.** Rooster
43. A Doughnut	**50.** Belt	**57.** Monkey
44. A Switch	**51.** Gymnast	**58.** Candle
45. A Strawberry	**52.** Sunglasses	**59.** River
46. Peacock	**53.** Boat	**60.** Darkness
47. Necktie	**54.** Shadow	**61.** Tomato
48. Paper	**55.** Plate	**62.** Stamp

Guess who or what I am ?

Chapter 1 - Answers

63. Giraffe	**70.** Onion	**77.** Window
64. Moon	**71.** Silence	**78.** Orange
65. Mushroom	**72.** A Doctor	**79.** Island
66. Boomerang	**73.** Money	**80.** Rat
67. T-Shirt	**74.** Kite	**81.** Snow
68. Traffic light	**75.** Dream	**82.** An Astronaut
69. Fan	**76.** Voice	**83.** Sheep

84. Brain	**90.** A Writer	**95.** A Butterfly
85. Blackboard	**91.** A Painter	**96.** Ears
86. Bee. Or honeybee	**92.** Snake	**97.** Plant
87. A Baby	**93.** Kidney	**98.** Clown
88. A Teacher	**94.** Bones.	**99.** The Queen
89. A Crocodile	Acceptable answer:	**100.** Dolphins
	Skeleton	**101.** Veterinarian

102. Soccer Player (Football for countries outside of the US)

103. Lion

104. Cactus

105. Policeman/policewoman

106. Chef

107. Singer

108. Hair

109. Lawyer

Chapter 2

Tricky Scenarios

"Knowledge will bring you the
opportunity to make
a difference."

~ Claire Fagan

Chapter 2 - Questions

1. There is a boat floating in the middle of the sea. At the side of the boat, there is a 10-foot ladder. The boat is fairly big, so the bottom of the ladder just touches the surface of the water. If the tide rises up at the rate of 8 inches per hour, how long will it take for half the ladder to be underwater?

2. A man went more than ten days without any sleep. How did he manage to do that?

3. A boy was dropped a real egg on a marble floor without cracking it. How is that possible?

4. A doctor hands you three pills. He gives you specific instructions to take the pills once every half an hour. How long would it take you to have all the pills?

5. It took ten men to build a wall. Six more men arrive to build the wall. How long will it take them?

Chapter 2 - Questions

6. M is the mother of B. But B is not the daughter of M. How is that possible?

7. How is it possible for you to lift an elephant with just one finger?

Chapter 2 - Questions

8. What is the most recent year you can think of when New Year's came before Christmas?

9. There are 144 turtles. Eight are on shore, and five of them drowned. How many turtles are left?

10. How many times do you think the letter 'a' appears in the number range from 1 to 100?

Chapter 2 - Questions

11. According to researchers, what do you find at the end of every rainbow?

12. There is a street that contains 100 houses. A sign-maker has been called in to create door numbers for the houses. Without using a calculator or other tools, how many 9's do you think he will need to create?

Chapter 2 - Questions

13. There is a person who does not have all his fingers on one hand. What do you call him?

14. Let's say that you place a cup on the table facing north. You then sit facing west. On which side can you find the cup's handle?

15. There are three rooms in a building. One of them contains a lot of gold. The second one contains many toys. The last room contains many bottles of water. One day, all three rooms caught fire. In which room did the policeman put out the fire first?

16. You have with you the number one. How do you make it disappear?

17. There were 14 birds on a tree. Susan scared away one bird. How many birds remained?

18. A ranger was in the forest and came upon 100 deer. With just a single shot, he got them all. How did he do it?

Chapter 2 - Questions

19. How many sides does a circle has?

20. What two word combination create the word with the most letters in the English language?

21. What was the President's name in 2011?

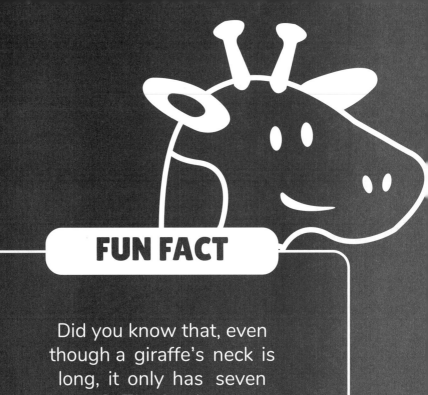

FUN FACT

Did you know that, even though a giraffe's neck is long, it only has seven bones? That's the same number of bones in a human's neck!

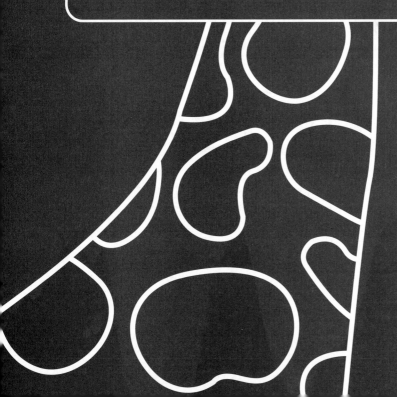

Chapter 2 - Questions

22. How can you spell the word "enemy" in three letters?

23. Is the capital of Australia spelled SIDNEY or SEDNEY?

24. In Bulgaria, no one is allowed to take a picture of a man with an eye patch. Why is that?

25. There is a particular coat that you need to use when it's wet. What coat is that?

Chapter 2 - Questions

26. How is it possible for a man to cut and tear other people's clothes, but they still thank him for it?

27. If John had six piles of sand and Adam added ten more piles, how many piles of sand will there be?

Chapter 2 - Questions

28. Look at the sequence of letters below. What are the next three letters in the sequence?

OTTFFSS

29. A teacher asked two boys the following questions:

a. Do you come from the same family?

b. Do you both have the same parents?

c. Do you both look alike?

d. Are you both twins?

The two boys said yes to questions a, b, and c. But they answered no to question d. How is that possible?

30. How much is the answer to this question. What is the answer to this question?

31. Two brothers, Jeremy and John, went to the park to play a game of chess. When they returned home, Jeremy told his mom that he played five games. John told his mom that he played six games. They are both telling the truth. How is that possible?

FUN FACT

You can fit more than a million Earths into the sun.

Chapter 2 - Questions

32. Why did a man ride a mule into the small town?

33. Which of the following words does not fit, and why?

Apple, Care, Strawberry

Chapter 2 - Questions

34. All of the words mentioned below have one thing in common except one. Can you find out the odd word?

a. bass   **b.** mark

b. console   **d.** produce

e. content   **f.** project

g. contest   **h.** record

i. desert   **j.** wind

35. All the words in the list below have the same unique feature. Can you find out what the unique feature is?

a. almost   **b.** below

c. first   **d.** glory

e. begin   **f.** empty

36. What common word in the English language contains the following sequence of letters (You are not allowed to use hyphens): C H C

37. There is a certain word in the English language. If you add a prefix to it, then the meaning of the word remains the same. (HINT: The word is related to fire).

Chapter 2 - Questions

38. Can you figure out what the sequence of characters mean in the arrangement below?

9 is the S R of 81

39. There are 195 countries in the world. But there are only two countries contain the letter 'X'. What countries are those?

40. The sequence of letters below have a meaning. Can you figure what the meaning is?

12 M in a Y

FUN FACT

A clock runs slightly
faster on a tall mountain
than it does at sea level.

Chapter 2 - Questions

41. There was one King standing against a horse. However, when the horse charged towards the King, it was the King that won. How is that possible?

42. A man is driving down the right. He then switches on the left indicator. However, when he turns, he turns right. He still does not manage to break any rules or do anything illegal. How is that possible?

Chapter 2 - Questions

43. A man created something strange that no one could see, not even him. What did he create?

44. There are 5 brothers and they are al lbusy. James is watching the television, Adam is reading a book, Rupert is playing tennis, and Benjamin is eating. What is the fifth brother doing?

Chapter 2 - Questions

45. How can you put an elephant into the refrigerator?

46. How can you put a giraffe into the refrigerator?

47. Two boys had entered a forest. It suddenly started raining really hard, so they took shelter in a small cave. When it stopped raining, they stepped out to hunt for food. Soon, they came to a fork in the road. One boy went left, and the second boy went right. The first boy came across an apple tree. Since he was hungry, he took a bite out of the apple. He was immediately transformed into an apple tree. The second boy went back to get his friend. A voice in the woods told him, "Your friend has been turned into an apple tree. If you can guess which tree is your friend, then he will return to normal, or else he will forever remain an apple tree." The second friend was able to guess which tree was his friend. How is that possible?

FUN FACT

The biggest flower in the world is found in Indonesia and it is bigger than a car tire! It is call the Rafflesia.

Chapter 2 - Questions

48. Sarah is standing behind Jenny, but Jenny is also standing behind Sarah. How is that possible?

49. What does this arrangement of letters mean?

Ban ana

50. What does the below arrangement of characters mean?

7 D in a W

Chapter 2 - Questions

51. Look at the arrangement of sports below. In what order are they arranged?

a. Golf   **b.** Tennis
b. Bowling   **d.** Basketball

52. A man jumped off a plane, but nothing happened to him. How is that possible?

53. A man taught his dog how to choose between red, yellow, blue, and green. After two years, he wanted to test the dog, but he found that the dog was unable to pick colors. Why?

54. If you are living near a freshwater lake, which of the below animals would you not be able to catch at all?

a. Otter   **b.** Alligator   **c.** Frog
d. Octopus   **e.** Beaver

55. There is a popular word associated with music that has no vowels. What word is that?

56. How many squares are there inside a cube?

Chapter 2 - Questions

57. If you bring a hot PAN and a CAKE together, what do you get?

58. A bottle of water was kept out in the hot sun, but the water did not evaporate. How is that possible?

59. If a frog has no legs, then what do you call it?

Chapter 2 - Questions

60. What five letter word starts and ends with the same letter and refers to something you have with your friend?

61. How can you split 3 potatoes between 5 people?

62. How is it possible that a ball of fire directly above you does not fall on you?

Chapter 2 – Questions

63. If it is 6:00 pm in England, then what time do you think it will be in Scotland?

64. If it is summer in Canada, then what season would it be in Australia?

FUN FACT

At any given point in time, clouds cover at least 60 percent of Earth!

Chapter 2 - Answers

1. It does not matter. If the tide rises, then so will the boat.

2. He went to sleep at night.

3. The egg cannot crack the marble floor.

4. Just one hour. You start by taking one pill immediately. Half an hour later, you can have the second pill. Another half hour later (at the one-hour mark), you can have the third pill.

5. None. The wall has already been built.

6. That is because B is the son of M.

7. It's not possible because you cannot find an elephant with just one finger.

8. This year. After all, New Year's always comes before Christmas.

9. All 144 turtles remain. Turtles cannot drown.

10. None. The letter 'a' does not appear at all in any of the numbers from 1 to 100.

11. The letter "w."

12. Twenty. From 1 to 89, there are nine 9s. 90 to 99 have eleven 9s. So a total of twenty 9s.

13. You call him a normal person. You only have half your fingers on one hand.

14. On the outside.

Chapter 2 - Answers

15. None of the rooms. Policemen do not put out fires.

16. You add the word G to it to make it "gone."

17. None. They all flew away.

18. He was taking a picture.

19. Just two actually. There is the inside and then there is the outside.

20. Post and office.

21. It hasn't changed. It was the same as it is today.

22. Foe.

23. Neither. The capital of Australia is Canberra.

24. You cannot take picture of anyone with an eyepatch. You need a camera.

25. It is a coat of paint.

26. That is because the man is a tailor.

27. One giant pile of sand.

28. ENT. They are the first letters for number one to ten.

29. That is because they are not twins. They are triplets. The third brother wasn't with them.

30. How much.

31. They were not playing the same games.

32. That is because he couldn't carry the mule.

Chapter 2 - Answers

33. The answer is strawberry because both apple and care end with an 'e' but strawberry does not.

34. All the words in the list can be pronounced in two different ways, except the word 'mark.'

35. The letters in the words are all arranged in alphabetical order.

36. Witchcraft

37. Flammable. If you turn it into inflammable, then the meaning remains the same.

38. 9 is the square root of 81.

39. Luxemburg and Mexico.

40. 12 months in a year.

41. It was a game of chess. It is possible for the King to overpower the horse (also called the knight)

42. The man had turned on the left indicator because he was going from the right lane to the left, even though he was turning right.

43. The man created noise.

44. The fifth brother is playing tennis with Rupert.

45. You simply open the door, place the elephant inside, and then close the door.

46. You can't. There is already an elephant in the refrigerator.

Chapter 2 - Answers

47. Since it had rained recently, the second friend look at the only tree that did not have any drops of water onit.

48. They are both standing back to back.

49. Banana split

50. 7 days in a week

51. They are arranged based on the size of the ball, with the golf ball being the smallest.

52. The plane was still on the ground. It hadn't taken off yet.

53. Dogs are colorblind.

54. Octopus. They do not live in freshwater.

55. Rhythm.

56. There are no squares inside a cube. They are all on the cube.

57. You get a cake that melts in the pan.

58. The bottle was not open.

59. Tadpole.

60. Trust.

61. You mash them. The mashed potatoes can be divided equally among 5 people.

62. It is because the ball of fire is the sun.

63. 6:00 PM. They are in the same time zone.

64. Winter.

Chapter 3

Guess
the Word!

"Creativity comes from trust. Trust
your instincts. And never hope more
than you work."

~ Rita Mae Brown

Chapter 3 - Questions

_ _ N _ _ _

1. This word is a king of roots. People use it when they are cooking something. It has a really strong taste.

What is it ?

_ _ A _ _ _ A _

2. It is used in BBQs! It is small and dark. You have to first heat it up until it catches fire.

What is it ?

_ _ _ A _ I _

3. It is a giant structure made of sand and stone. You find it in the desert. There are three versions of it. The structure itself is found in a country in Africa.

What is it ?

_ I _ _ _ I _ _

4. It has many hands, but they don't meet. You can usually find it in a farm. It is a large structure, and it uses the wind to generate power.

What is it ?

Chapter 3 - Questions

_ _ P _ _ _ R

5. It is a planet. In fact, it is much larger than Earth. It is close to the asteroid belt.

What is it ?

_ _ _ _ A _ O _

6. It is a type of machine. If you would like to get to the top of a building or if you would like to get down to the ground floor, then you would need this machine. Sometimes, the machine has a lot of space. Other times, not so much. You do to press buttons to reach your destination.

What is it ?

Chapter 3 - Questions

_ _ O _ _ C _

7. If you are going to eat food, then you are need this. Once your food goes down your throat, it ends up in this place. In fact, all the animals have it too.

What is it ?

_ _ O _ _ I _ _

8. If you come across this creature in the wild, then make sure that you do not go near it. It has a long tail that it is not afraid to use. The smaller ones are more dangerous than the bigger ones.

What is it ?

Chapter 3 - Questions

_ _ _ **E** _ _ _ _ **O** _

9. It has a green exterior and a red interior. It is not a plant. In fact, it is something that you can eat. Be careful, however. It has so many seeds.

What is it ?

_ _ **E** _ _ _ _ _

10. It has a trunk, but it is not a tree. You can find it in the wild, but you don't find it alone. It loves to spray water on itself to keep it cool during the summer.

What is it ?

_ **I** _ _ **O** _ _

11. It helps you remember the past. It helps you know what happened to a particular person, country, or event. You can learn about events that happened 50 years ago or 500 years ago.

What is it ?

_ _ _ **C** _ _ _ **I** _ _

12. It is used to scratch against a surface. But when you scratch it, it creates a flame. It looks like a really small stick. Usually, it is wooden.

What is it ?

Chapter 3 - Questions

_ _ _ _ **U** _ _

13. It is a planet, but it is also a liquid. You can find the liquid in many thermometers to measure temperature.

What is it ?

_ _ **N** _ _ _ _ _ _ **I** _ **T** _

14. It is present on all our fingers. You have it, but there is nobody else in the world that has the same type as you do. It can be used to identify us.

What is it ?

Chapter 3 - Questions

_ _ _ _ E _ _ _

15. You need it when it rains to keep you dry. If you want to avoid getting wet, then make sure that you take it with you.

What is it ?

_ _ _ C _ _ _

16. It is something you have as a snack. It makes popping noises when you are cooking it. You can usually find it when you visit a movie theatre.

What is it ?

FUN FACT

Did you know that raspberries, peaches, apples, plums, pears, and even cherries are all part of the family of roses? These fruits all belong to the Rosaceae family.

Chapter 3 - Questions

_ A _ _ _

17. It is a popular Italian dish, but you can find it all over the world. It usually comes with tomato sauce but there are many ways to prepare it.

What is it ?

_ _ _ _ B _ _ _ _ E _

18 . These are a type of fruit. They are berries, and they are quite popular around the world. They usually have a red or maroon shade, and then can be quite sweet. They are truly good for your health.

What is it ?

_ _ _ _ I _

19 . If you would like to create words, then you might need me. I am commonly used in schools, but people who would like to draw something also use me. I also come in different colors.

What is it ?

_ U _ _ _ _

20. It moves around with a house on its back. Do not frighten it, or it might withdraw into its house. It does not move too fast. It can come out on land, and it can swim underwater.

What is it ?

Chapter 3 - Questions

_ _ _ U _ _

21. At this time of the year the leaves fall from the trees. It can be hot and then it can turn really cold. You might even notice some leaves turn yellow during this time of the year.

What is it ?

_ _ _ _ U _ I _ _

22. It has so many needles, but you don't use it to make clothes. Don't go near it, or it might poke you with those needles. You can find it in the wild, although some people keep it at home as a pet. **What is it ?**

Chapter 3 - Questions

_ _ _ _ O _

23. You are a flat surface, but it is not a table. If you look into it, then you can find yourself looking back. You can find it in your bathroom or in many clothing stores.

What is it?

_ E _ _ _ _ I _ _

24. It is a type of sea animal. Surprisingly, it does not have fins or gills. It floats around slowly. It can be really colorful, but you should not come close to it. You might get stung!

What is it?

_ _ O _ A _ _

25. It is a fruit that is quite popular around the world. It has a soft exterior and a hard center. You have to usually scoop out the large seed before you have the fruit. The fruit itself has a green color.

What is it?

_ O _ _ A _ _

26. It is a type of wind that goes round and round. If you look at it, then it might remind you of a tall pillar. However, be careful that you do not go close to it, since it can cause a lot of destruction.

What is it?

FUN FACT

You might think that tigers only have striped fur. But that is not true at all. They also have striped skin.

Chapter 3 - Questions

_ _ _ I _ _ _

27. You find it in the wild. It walks just like human beings do. It is big and hairy. It can easily climb trees, but you usually find it on the ground.

What is it?

_ _ _ U _ _ _ _ E

28. Whenever you suffer an injury, or when you have an emergency, then you need to get to the hospital. When you do, you need this vehicle to take you there. You might recognize its familiar sirens when you hear it in the distance.

What am I ?

Chapter 3 - Questions

_ _ L _ _ _ _ _ E

29. When it starts to ring, then you have to answer it. You can use it to talk to people really far away from you.

What am I ?

_ E _ _ _ C _ _ _

30. You may not be able to see the stars up close. But you can use a tool for that purpose. This object allows you to see distance objects, whether they are on land or up in the sky. Scientists use this tool to look at objects in space.

What am I ?

Chapter 3 - Answers

1.	Ginger	6.	Elevator
2.	Charcoal	7.	Stomach
3.	Pyramid	8.	Scorpion
4.	Windmill	9.	Watermelon
5.	Jupiter	10.	Elephant

11.	History	16.	Popcorn
12.	Matchstick	17.	Pasta
13.	Mercury	18.	Cranberries
14.	Fingerprints	19.	Pencil
15.	Umbrella	20.	Turtle

21.	Autumn	26.	Tornado
22.	Porcupine	27.	Gorilla
23.	Mirror	28.	Ambulance
24.	Jellyfish	29.	Telephone
25.	Avocado	30.	Telescope

Chapter 4

Lost in Sentences!

"Learning is a treasure that will follow its owner everywhere."

~ Chinese Proverbs

Chapter 4 - Questions

Use the letters to spell out the answers to the clues.

HINT: Most answers are common phrases and sayings!

1. AEVH OENSDC UGHOHTST

The first word is used to refer to something that you hold or own. The second word is a measurement of time. The third word is something your mind creates. When all the words are combined, it is a phrase you use when you are doubtful about something.

2. DRAE TEEENWB HET EINLS

The first word in the sentence is an activity that you do to get more knowledge. The last word refers things that you can draw from point A to point B. When four words are combined, the sentence means that you must find the hidden meaning!

3.   SORSC UROY RGSINFE

You can make this action with just one hand. When it is done, it resembles a knot. You do it when you want to wish for good luck.

4.   EYRG AERA

One of the words is a color. The other word refers to a piece of land. The two words form a sentence that means something that is not clear.

Chapter 4 - Questions

5. DAD ULEF OT HET IERF

The first word in the sentence is a way you find the total of two or more numbers. The last word in the sentence is a chemical reaction that can create light. The entire sentence refers to something that means a situation is being made worse.

6. OLOC SA A UECMURCB

The first word refers to a state of temperature. The last word refers to a green vegetable that is part of the melon family. The phrase means someone is calm.

Chapter 4 - Questions

7. YUSB SA A EBE

The first word indicates a situation where you have so much to do and you are completely occupied. The last word is a flying insect that is nature's friend. When you combine four words, then the sentence means that you are working hard,or you are very active.

8. EPSIPLD YM IDNM

The first word refers to a situation where you lose balance. The last word is what your brain creates to help you think. When you combine three words, then you create a sentence that you use when you forget something.

Chapter 4 - Questions

9. ISFH UTO FO ARWET

The first word is a creature that does not have any lungs! The last word is something that covers the Earth in large quantities. When you combine four words, then the sentence refers to a situation where you are in a place you don't belong.

---

10. ODLH URYO OSHESR

The first word in the sentence is an action where you grab on to something. The final word is a creature that has a long face and can run fast. When three words combine, they form a sentence you can use to tell someone to wait a minute!

---

11. YCR ORDLEOCIC ERSTA

The first word refers to something you do when you are sad. The second word refers to a large reptile. When you combine three words, then you form a sentence that means a person is pretending to be upset.

---

12. A ITLTLE IRDIBE OTDL EM

The second word means something that is really small. The fourth word is the past tense of tell. When you combine five words, then you create a sentence that means that someone told you a secret!

FUN FACT

Did you know that the
sea cucumber breathes
through its butt?

13. ETG DOLC ETEF

The second word is a state of the temperature. The last word is a part of your body that helps you walk properly. When you combine three words, then you create a sentence that means that you are nervous.

14. SAPS IHWT YIFGNL OLRCSO

The first word is used when you succeed on a test. The third word is an action taken by winged creatures. The last word is created by light and makes the world vibrant. This phrase is used when someone has done very well or has been successful with an achievement.

Chapter 4 - Questions

15. ILFL NI HET LKSABN

The first word is something that you do when you want to fill a container full. The last word refers to something that is empty. When you combine the four words, then you get a sentence that means you should provide more information.

---

16. LCLA TI A YDA

The first word is something that you do when you pick up the phone. The last word is a time when the sun is up. When you combine four words, then you form a sentence that you use when you want to indicate that it is time to stop or quit.

---

17. SA HIWET SA A OTGHS

The second word is a kind of color that is formed when all colors in the color spectrum combine. The last word refers to something spooky. When you combine five words, then you form a sentence that means that someone is truly frightened, or their complexion is pale.

---

18. IEHV FO TYICAIVT

The first word refers to a large colony where creatures live and make honey. The last word refers to something that requires action. When three words combine, they form a sentence that refers to a busy place, whether at your school or at home.

Chapter 4 - Questions

19. PSIN A RANY

The first word refers to an action where you go round and round. The last work is a material used in sewing clothes. When three words combine, they refer to the act of telling a long and quite a far-fetched story.

20. RIGGWLE IEKL A ROWM

The first word is an action that you take when you want to squeeze through a narrow space. The last word refers to a creature that lives underground and has no eyes, no hands, and no legs. When four words are combined, you get a sentence that refers to an action where you move like an underground creature.

Chapter 4 - Questions

21. RANW OEMOSNE FOF

The first word refers to an action that you take in order to tell someone that they are going to face danger. The last word is the opposite of 'on.' When three words combine, they form a phrase that refers to the action of alerting someone of danger.

22. IGNARIN TCAS DAN DSGO

The first word is what happens when the sky is dark. The second word is a kind of creature you wouldn't mind having in your house. When you combine the four words, you form a sentence that means that it is pouring heavily outside.

23. AHEV A NGHACE FO ERAHT

The third word means shifting from one form to another. The last word is an organ that is important for survival. When you combine five words, you make a sentence that means a person has changed his mind.

24. ECNOSD OT OENN

The first word is a position that you attain if you are not leading the pack. The last word means not a single person or thing. When you combine all three words, then you for a phrase that you use to refer to someone who is the best!

Chapter 4 - Questions

25. LALT YSROT

The first word is a way to describe someone's height. The second word is something that has a lot of words and takes you to magical places. When two words combine, they form a phrase that refers to a tale that is quite hard to believe.

26. CIING NO HTE KCEA

The first word refers to something that you add on top of desserts. The last word is something that completes your birthday. When you combine four words, the sentence means something that is added to make things great!

27. ELFL NO EFAD RESA

The first word is what happens when a person tripped on something. The third word is a condition where someone is not able to hear you. When you combine four words, then the sentence means that even though you were trying to say something, people were not listening to you.

28. ATC OTG URYO UETNO G?

The second word is used when you receive something. The last word is a part of the body that helps you check whether your food is sweet or not. When you combine four words, you get the question you ask when someone isn't talking or when someone cannot respond to you.

FUN FACT

Did you know that the creature with the largest eyes is the Giant Squid? Its eyes can grow to be 10 inches in diameter. In other words, its eyes can become as big as your head!

Chapter 4 - Answers

1. Have Second Thoughts

2. Read Between the Lines

3. Cross Your Fingers

4. Grey Area

5. Add Fuel to the Fire

6. Cool as a Cucumber

7. Busy as a Bee

8. Slipped My Mind

9. Fish Out of Water

10. Hold Your Horses

---

11. Cry Crocodile Tears

12. A Little Birdie Told Me

13. Get Cold Feet

14. Pass with Flying Colors

15. Fill in The Blanks

16. Call it a Day

17. As White as a Ghost

18. Hive of Activity

19. Spin a Yarn

20. Wriggle Like a Worm

---

21. Warn Someone Off

22. Raining Cats and Dogs

23. Have a Change of Heart

24. Second to None

25. Tall Story

26. Icing on the Cake

27. Fell on Deaf Ears

28. Cat Got Your Tongue?

Did you enjoy the book?

If you did, we are ecstatic. If not, please write your complaint to us and we will ensure we ix it.

If you're feeling generous, there is something important that you can help me with – tell other people that you enjoyed the book.

Ask a grown-up to write about it on Amazon. When they do, more people will find out about the book. It also lets Amazon know that we are making kids around the world laugh. Even a few words and ratings would go a long way.

If you have any ideas or jokes that you think are super funny, please let us know. We would love to hear from you. Our email address is -

riddleland@riddlelandforkids.com

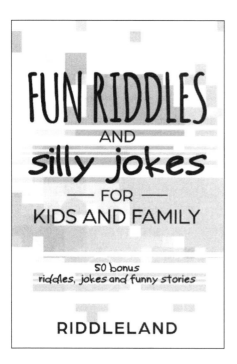

https://pixelfy.me/riddlelandbonus

Thank you for buying this book. We would like to share
a special bonus as a token of appreciation.
It is a collection of 50 original jokes, riddles, and
two funny stories

CONTEST

Would you like your jokes and riddles to be featured in our next book?

We are having a contest to see who are the smartest or funniest boys and girls in the world!

1) Creative and Challenging Riddles
2)Tickle Your Funny Bone Contest

Parents, please email us your child's "original" Riddle or Joke, **and he or she could win a $25 Amazon gift card and be featured in our next book.**

Here are the rules:

1) It must be challenging for the riddles and funny for the jokes!

2) It must be 100% original and not something from the Internet! It is easy to find out!

3) You can submit both a joke and a riddle as they are two separate contests.

4) No help from the parents unless they are as funny as you.

5) Winners will be announced via email or our Facebook group – Riddleland for kids

6) Please also mention what book you purchased.

7) Email us at Riddleland@riddlelandforkids.com

Other Fun Books By Riddleland
Riddles Series

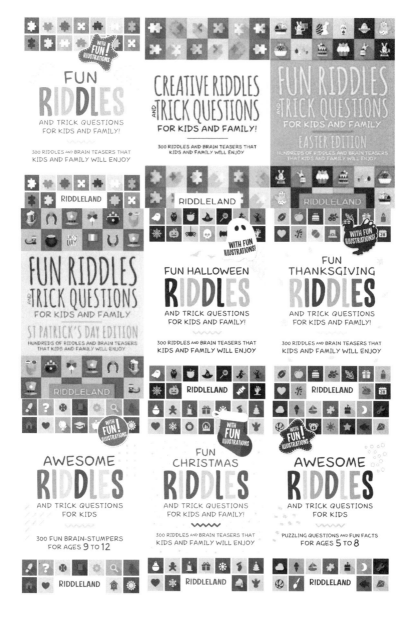

Try Not to Laugh Challenge
Joke Series

Would You Rather Series

Get them on Amazon or our website at
www.riddlelandforkids.com

About Riddleland

Riddleland is a mum + dad run publishing company. We are passionate about creating fun and innovative books to help children develop their reading skills and fall in love with reading. If you have suggestions for us or want to work with us, shoot us an email at

riddleland@riddlelandforkids.com

Our family's favorite quote

"Creativity is an area in which younger people have a tremendous advantage since they have an endearing habit of always questioning past wisdom and authority."

– Bill Hewlett.

References

Ref :

DK. (2017). DK children's encyclopedia. - DKChildren.